Concertina

MERCER
UNIVERSITY PRESS

Endowed by
TOM WATSON BROWN
and
THE WATSON-BROWN FOUNDATION, INC.

Concertina

Poems

Joseph Bathanti

Mercer University Press
Macon, Georgia

MUP/ P480

© 2013 Mercer University Press
1400 Coleman Avenue
Macon, Georgia 31207

First Edition

Books published by Mercer University Press are printed on acid-free paper that
meets the requirements of the American National Standard for Information
Sciences—Permanence of Paper for Printed Library Materials.

Mercer University Press is a member of Green Press Initiative
(greenpressinitiative.org), a nonprofit organization working to help publishers
and printers increase their use of recycled paper and decrease their use of fiber
derived from endangered forests. This book is printed on recycled paper.
Library of Congress Cataloging-in-Publication Data

Bathanti, Joseph.
  [Poems. Selections]
  Concertina : Poems / Joseph Bathanti. -- First Edition.
    pages cm
  ISBN 978-0-88146-470-2 (paperback : acid-free paper) –
  ISBN 0-88146-470-8 (paperback : acid-free paper)
  I. Title.
  PS3602.A89C66 2013
  811'.6--dc23
                          2013030159

Acknowledgments

Grateful acknowledgment is extended to the following journals in which some of these poems, in some cases different versions, first appeared:

"Flate" in *Aethlon*; "Doughnuts," "The Sick Room," and "Teaching an Inmate to Read" in *Birmingham Poetry Review*; "Inmates Working" in *Blue Mesa Review*; "Home" and "Cletis Pratt" in *Café Solo*; "The City Jail" in *The Dead Mule School of Southern Literature*; "The Dogs at Salisbury," "Jury Duty," and "Sweet Random" in *New Letters*; "Crying" in *Ecotone*; "Raskolnikov" in *Greenfield Review*; "Shank" in *Florida Humanities*; "Night and Fog" in *Poetry International*; "Three Little Pigs" in *Pembroke Magazine*; "Huron Valley" and "Poetry" in *Platte Valley Review*; "Certainty," Huntersville Prison," and "This Mad Heart" in *Poet Lore*; "Freedom Drive" and "Recidivism" in *Prison Arts Coalition Blog*; "The Footlocker" in *The Progressive*; "Praise the Lord" in *Rattle*; "Concertina," "Robert Lowell," and "Women's Prison" in *Shenandoah*; "Transfer Day" in *Tar River Poetry*; "Drayfer's Last Number" and "Prison AA," in *Town Creek Poetry*; "Faccia Tosta," "Teddy Bear," and "The Wall" in *The Sun*.

"Raskolnikov" appeared in the chapbook, *The Feast of All Saints* (Nightshade Press, 1994).

Thanks also to the anthologies and their editors in which the following poems appeared: "Cletis Pratt" in *I Go to the Ruined Place: Contemporary Poems in Defense of Global Human Rights*; "That Good Old Way" in *The Sound of Poets Cooking*.

"Cletis Pratt" is the winner of the 2007 Barbara Mandigo Kelly Peace Poetry Prize, awarded annually by the Nuclear Age Peace Foundation in Santa Barbara, California. The poem was also published on the Foundation's website.

For Joan: from the first day

Contents

Concertina

The Footlocker

The day before I left Pittsburgh
to work as a VISTA Volunteer
in the prisons of North Carolina,
my father drove me in the family car—

an enormous two-door green Chrysler Newport—
downtown to the Army-Navy store on Liberty Avenue.
He was set on buying me a footlocker,
something I had never dreamt of possessing,

to pack everything I'd be taking.
He and my mother were befuddled as to why I—
having recently earned a Master's Degree—
wished to spend my days among criminals

500 miles from home for $2000 a year.
They had little faith in my car,
a beat-up 69 VW Bug with no reverse.
My mother wept. My father said nothing.

In my recollection, he has never attempted
to dissuade me from anything, nor made public his desires,
two things for which I can't begin to express my gratitude.
I didn't want a footlocker,

but couldn't bring myself to tell him so.
We wandered the store looking at switchblades,
gas masks, live grenades, then purchased the footlocker.
My dad wanted to get me something else.

→

Realizing a refusal would be unkind,
I picked out a denim cowboy shirt with pearl buttons—
at the time a real stretch for me.
But, in twenty-four hours, I'd walk away from my past.

Style seemed irrelevant. Next door
to the Army-Navy sprawled a string of porno shops.
Once, I snuck into one with a friend.
We squeezed into a booth and watched a 25-cent

black and white clip, then gaped at magazine jackets,
contraptions and novelties that belonged in a laboratory.
A black curtain through which men passed
in and out led to a back room.

Such experiences, I'm certain, are not unusual
among boys. Yet, standing that day
on Liberty Avenue with my father,
I was filled not with shame, but regret—

because I was leaving and glad about it.
I didn't require absolution,
but I longed to tell him about slipping into that dive.
For all I know—and I realize now how little

I knew about the inside of my father—
he too had been in one of those places before.
But it was painful thinking about having
 something like this in common with my dad,

and I valued above all else—and I think he did too—
that we never spoke of such things.
I was 23 years old; and that fact,
in the line of men I issued from,

entitled me to my silence.
My father and I climbed back into the Chrysler
and drove home to my mother and the last supper
we would ever eat together

on that still green side of my life.
The next morning, I picked up I-79
and headed south. In the backseat
of my car lay the footlocker

which I still own and use to store
old manuscripts, notebooks and letters
that in all likelihood
I'll never return to.

Crying

*Convicts of all races frequently have teardrops
tattooed directly below their eyes, giving them the
appearance of permanently crying.*
　　　　　　　—Andrew Lichtenstein

He's a poor white kid from nowhere,
a little X in Anson County called Cairo,
half ghost town: a few trailers,
amnesiac farmsteads, forsaken croplands

shanked into the Chesterfield County line,
South Carolina. Doing his time here
at Huntersville, he's only 70 or so miles from home,
but home might as well be Cairo, Egypt.

He'll never see his folks again.
None of them can read or write,
the car seized up and chocked
in the demented swales long ago.

He's probably just old enough by a day
to fetch adult time in an adult camp.
Bad luck. No guardian angel.
No cross to lift him.

Wouldn't know a crucifix
were it pounded through his heart.
Scraps of black down stitch his lip and chin.
He'd fall apart in his mama's arms.

Off to himself, on the yard, at a picnic table
under one of the big shedding oaks, with a cigarette,
gazing at the evergreens on the other side
of Mount Holly-Huntersville Road

—the free side of steel,
just a few feet beyond where he sits,
smoke clouding about him.
The guys wear their coats snapped,

hands pocketed. Turn their backs,
and lean into what's ahead:
maybe Christmas.
Christmas is free to everyone.

This kid: collar hiked, one of those Castro
Honor-Grade green caps pulled over
his square white forehead, black
brow. Tattooed beneath his left eye

is a single blue teardrop,
needled into him—in a Salisbury Street
shothouse? Deese's Speakeasy?
A Sugartown crackhouse? No telling.

Or how he found his way into one of them.
The bad shit has a way of democratizing itself.
He says he doesn't know why he did it.
He doesn't know why he's done anything.

Concertina

Alias razor wire, fashioned after
the free-reed,
bellows-drive instrument, patented

in 1844 by
Sir Charles Wheatstone. Early in its history,
Rimsky-Korsakov's

Flight of the Bumblebee was arranged for English
concertina.
Used as ramparts in WWI. You've seen

archival photographs
of soldiers dangling still, lovelorn, as puppets
in its trusses.

Simple barbed wire garnished with spun helices of high
tensile yield,
various calibers and blade profiles, a colossal Slinky

ribboned with scalpels
that incise vertically and horizontally at once.
An Italian Squeezebox.

Manufacturers' names like *Excalibur, Flight-Guard, Whistler,
Nemesis, The Prodigal*—
so conceived that, once snared, the convict, reflexively

thrashing (panicked
as it flinches into him), ravels himself through
a meat grinder.

In the sun and moonlight, especially seductive.
The intermezzo,
the climactic hemorrhage.

Sweet Random

That first week on the project,
the four of us new VISTAs crashed
at our boss's cramped flat:

a Jewish girl from Bayonne; a Cuban
whose preacher father was locked
in Castro's Havana jail; a girl

from Atlanta; and I, a Catholic
from Pittsburgh. Crammed together
as we were—hot as fire,

no air-conditioning—at night,
we drank outside, smoldering,
as if on the brink of razing every prison

in North Carolina. One day, after
a long fruitless search for my own place,
the Atlanta girl, Joan Carey, emerged

from the tiny bathroom, wrapped
in a towel, chestnut hair pinned
atop her head, into the full early

evening sun blazing through
the windows. The towel: buttery
gold with wheat stalks in full

blond raiment, clouds of pale
chaff in the pollinated light of what
would be another long sultry

August night in Charlotte. She and I,
up to that point, had been friendly,
even circumspectly affectionate.

Dazed by the sight of her in nothing
but a towel, the sun stealing
over us, I knew little

of her, perhaps less of myself,
purely nothing of the lives
of caged men. I envisioned

prison as Purgatory,
a colossal furnace hoarding
chits on me. Above all,

so help me God, I felt blessed
by those shackled men pulling my time
in the forge. Forsaking home

for toil among convicts,
it had been rectitude I desired:
an apparition bare and reckoning

as an angel with a flaming sword.
Ahead of me beckoned sweet random;
all night I held it seared against me.

Doughnuts

There seemed little danger the evening I stood
the first time in the freakish August heat
on a prison yard: Mount Pleasant,
a minimum security camp deep

in Cabarrus County cropland.
It had a domestic tranquility.
The guards wore street clothes, no guns,
just an aerosol of mace and tiny blackjack.

The visiting area was a cluster
of picnic tables and pastel sun umbrellas.
In the center of the yard, inmates,
like schoolboys, shirtless, in cut-off honor

grade trousers, figure-eighted a slab of concrete
between two steel-netted hoops, some in State-
issue Keds, others barefoot.
The comforting thud of the ball on concrete,

the peel of it off the rim.
Names like Popcorn, Popeye, Q-Tip, Puddin',
Hungry Bull, Lump, Shake'n'Bake—an endearing docket
of innocent aliases. Laughing,

chattering as they played, their crimes seemed
irrelevant, even imagined.
An unfastened padlock hung querulously
in its hasp on the front gate. There was nothing

to keep them from simply ambling off—
the chain-link fence threatless as the one
circling my kindergarten schoolyard.
The dew had already welled

in the endless spermy free green
distant swales: jasmine, Joe Pye, jewel weed,
clusters of black cows, mammoth spools of hay.
Fugitive cascades of kudzu strangled the trees.

Mount Pleasant's captain was Clyde Stillman:
a grey head of white wire bristle.
An oscillating fan on a pole lashed
over him behind a big oak desk, maroon

pants and shirt, a shade off from each other.
A cowboy hat hung from a hook. He rolled
one-handed with ungummed Bugler skins
and a red, rusted tin of Prince Albert crimp-cut,

hawked into a cuspidor atop his desk,
struck the blue-tip match off the block wall.
We shook hands. He asked where I went to church,
slipped me a pocket tract called *The Great News*,

from the International Bible Society:
three black crosses barbed across its red face.
There came a knock at the screen door.
Behind it, an ancient African

convict in cook's whites snatched
his cap from his head and covered his heart.
In his other hand rested a plate of doughnuts.
"Captain," he invoked, eyes on the ground –   →

waited like that outside in the yard
until Stillman allowed, "Boy," a shroud
of tobacco smoke attending the hushed
syllable—then tripped into the office,

set the doughnuts on the desk next to the spittoon,
departed silently without looking up,
the warm scent lifting off them, the still-wet
glaze glistening, pooling at the plate edge.

Night and Fog

(after the film by Alain Resnais)

It's an old print, black
and white, spidered, spliced,
as though shot through gossamer.

The film chops through the projector
sprockets and pulleys and splays
itself on the Ed trailer wall.

Bulldozers shove corpses into craters.
Naked, spindly, like dolls,
the same wooden apathy, arms

and legs tangling as they tumble in.
The inmates can't believe it.
What is this shit?

Who made this movie?
Outside it's raining.
The yardmen carry umbrellas

and wear long black State macks,
emblazoned *Department of Correction*
yellow on their backs.

When the film clatters to a halt
there is for a moment the white square
of light, cigarette smoke

→

coiling through it, then just the black
trailer wall and the glow of the yard
lights profiling the prisoners.

Freedom Drive

At Camp Greene, I picked up two inmates rigged out in street clothes for work-release interviews at Jack's Steak House on Freedom Drive. A petite convict named Short Dog, all mouth, never stopped, the almighty dozens—what the inmates termed *jooging*—a nervous conspiratorial laugh, toothpick, black leather jacket, and black toboggan. Like a warhead. And a husky woman I had never seen before: Debbie, from the Halfway House on Park Road. Garish make-up, close afro, decked in hot pants, platforms, skimpy red tube cinching her considerable breasts, yet practiced in her dainty airs.

She and Short Dog lounged in the back seat of the state car: a blue '74 Valiant that bore the North Carolina Department of Correction decal on its front doors: a downward arrow that suddenly U-turned Heavenward, symbolic of the restoration engendered by a stretch in prison—the DOC at its most allegorical. The car had a bright yellow commonwealth tag and a CB that was to remain engaged whenever the vehicle was in operation. Along the drive shaft was a bracket to rack and lock a shotgun. I had switched off the CB. We listened to the radio. Autumn of '76, Dylan's *Desire:* "Hurricane" and "Joey." The inmates liked those songs—the blood and danger.

We plopped in a booth at Jack's. Debbie, red lipsticked mouth, batting eyes, blush caked on her high brown cheeks, propped her big breasts on the Formica—a carnal chain gang icon—Short Dog grinning gaudily, balancing the shaker in a drift of salt, worrying that toothpick around his mouth like a compass needle. The manager asked them a few questions, and hired them on the spot. Inmate labor was cheap and dependable.

On the way back to the camp, they smoked cigarettes, and held hands. We dropped by the Dairy Queen and together slowly ate the white pristine cones. Short Dog, later on the yard, finally clued me

15

that Debbie was no girl, but Dwight, a transsexual, not the same as a he-she, but an inmate who had crossed over prior to going down; therefore the State was obliged by law to keep the hormones coming and everything else, including, if and when, the irrevocable surgery.

Debbie—everyone called her *the girl* — wore Honor Grade fatigues on the yard, but come lock-down shed to teddies and camisoles, a straight-up female—you couldn't tell the difference—with a vicious body and lingerie living in the penitentiary dorm with 180 men who hadn't had a woman in years. And she fought like a gladiator.

Convicts arriving on the transfer bus figured they'd caught the best time on the State. A nightmare for custody, the Department didn't know how to classify her, what pronoun was appropriate. Technically she was not a woman, so they couldn't transfer her to Women's in Raleigh. She was clearly not a man.

I didn't know a damn thing, and that was never more apparent than that afternoon on Freedom Drive when I could not distinguish a man from a woman. I was just driving the car, digging Dylan, and a 50-cent cone from the DQ. In fact, I had been thinking: *Mother of God.* But not a desperate or even imploring *Mother of God.* Rather, a prayer of thanksgiving, near euphoria, that my life was just starting and the world was so utterly strange.

The Wall

Joan and I were in Raleigh together
for the first time to take the tour
for new VISTA volunteers
at North Carolina's Central Prison,

a hundred years old, built by convict labor
along the railroad tracks behind Morgan Street
so new felons could be shipped in by boxcar.
The inmates called it *The Wall*:

1300 of them locked down.
Guards with Tommy guns
manned the towers 24 hours.
The fence that crowned the high stone

perimeter was electrified.
We were marched right into the gut of it:
I and J blocks, where the criminally insane,
playing badminton on an asphalt court

wrapped in glittering silver concertina,
screamed obscenities at the girls. A wall
with bullet holes in it. No buttons
in the elevators, just an intercom and a camera.

The Death House, in a grassy side yard
spilling with pink primrose, had to be entered
through a heavy church door. Inside
lurked the gas chamber: an oak chair bolted

→

17

to the floor in a glassed confessional.
A row of red-cushioned pews for the witnesses.
Though mid-August, Death Row was cold.
Joan wore my green flannel shirt,

her long brown hair still damp from bathing.
I had known her only a week.
In college she'd played piano for prisoners
at the Dekalb County Jail in Atlanta.

The Central condemned wore white: white
beltless trousers, white tucked-in shirts.
They were barefoot, washed in light.
We filed past their cells along a narrow

gunmetal catwalk hung over an abyss.
We couldn't see bottom.
As Joan queued along the tier—
her head was down—

the men milled to the fronts of their cells
and clenched the bars,
mere likenesses of one another,
amnesiacs, ghostly in their whites,

that odd gleam pooled about them—
not wholly there, but evanescent,
while we hovered trying,
not to face them in midair.

The Dogs at Salisbury

The bloodhounds were caged in a skirmish of wire lots—
the same wire that penned the convicts—
along the left field line of the Salisbury camp
softball field in Rowan County.
Doped and clumsy, the dogs paced
their tiny allotments, waiting
to be sprung on the trail
of some wayfaring booster turned rabbit.

The penitentiary contracted an old fire-
faced free man named Luther
to run down escapes they couldn't collar
once into deep country.
Bounty hunter's what he amounted to.
Went horseback: convict Stetson hat,
khaki work fatigues, cartridge belt, and pistol.
An awful throwback man, and no believer.

A band of lifers, dog-boys, so-called,
strange and beholden to Luther, tetched
from too long in jail, ran, on all fours
if need be, with him on the track of an escape.
They babied those dogs like lovers,
loosed them on long chains, and swabbed their faces
with the ratty tattered gray bunk-clothes
their prey had slipped out of just before
dawn shift change among the guards.

Luther cantered up on a sorrel gelding,
rolled a tailor-made from a can of Stud.
Sat there in a scud of smoke,
then wordlessly led them out.   →

It had a stylized filmic tint to it,
but stripped of movie stars and allegory:
just shackle and Leviticus;
the infernal antebellum geography,
impenetrable wet burning green;
Luther, his catamites, and a pack
of chain gang bloodhounds,
their obscene shimmy and piss,
the slavering coiled bray,
Jesus dragging his tree
through swamp and nightshade.

Teaching an Inmate to Read

At a yard picnic table,
I'm teaching Mickey Rooney,
whose real name I've forgotten,
to read with flashcards I hold
before his astonished face:
cat (paired with a picture
of a yellow tabby), *dog*
(a Springer spaniel).
We sound out the words,
exaggerating each vowel,
each consonant, the way I remember
being taught in first grade by Sister Sarah—
a few syllables to get him down the road
if ever the gate swings open.

From Transylvania County,
he has a mild form of Down syndrome,
high cheekbones, haunting Oriental eyes –
gorgeous hazel almonds,
irises flecked with white known
as Brushfield spots—that render him
Mandarin. With an IQ of 70
he's "borderline, high-functioning,"
classified as "socially retarded,"
his tragic flaw the presence
of an extra 21st chromosome,
the smallest human chromosome.
He's down this jolt for swiping
a Muscular Dystrophy can
from Piggly Wiggly.

→

He volunteers that every night at lockdown
another convict on the block is dogging him
and the guards won't step in.
Rape, he's confiding — this other guy
forcing Mickey to go down on him,
a whole grab bag of other plays too.
"Ain't nothin'," he mutters. Smokes a cigarette,
wears a cap of yellow hair,
kind of smiles, his tongue lashing up
to touch his little nose at intervals,
like it really is nothing and my job's simply
to listen and not be shocked, shrug it off
while this kid gets punked night after night —
as if it's a story he's locked in,
not a penitentiary, and he's a character
immured in his own primer.

With childish wonderment,
Mickey whizzes through the drills:
Mother (Betty Crocker,
pert as gingham, fluoride smile),
Father (happy white guy
in a blue suit, Bryl Cream and briefcase),
Home (a red house, smoke
penciling out of its chimney).

Women's Prison

Two Sundays a month, darkness still abroad,
we round up the kids and bundle them
into a restored salvaged Bluebird school bus,
repainted green, and make the long haul

to Raleigh where their mothers are locked
in Women's Prison. We pin the children's names
and numbers to their coats, count them
like convicts at lights-out. Sucking thumbs,

clutching favorite oddments to cuddle as they ride
curled in twos on patched sprung benches,
they sleepwalk bashfully, the little aged,
into the belly of the bus, eyes nailed to its floor.

We feed them milk and juice, animal crackers, apples;
stop for them to use the bathroom,
and to change the ones so young, they can't help wetting.
We try singing: folk tunes and strike ballads—

as if off to picket or march with an army of babies—
but their stony faces will not yield and, finally,
their passion to disappear puts them to sleep,
not to wake until the old Bluebird jostles

through the checkpoints into the prison.
Somehow, upon reopening their eyes, they know
to smile at the twirling jagged grandeur
surrounding the massive compound: concertina—

→

clotted with silver scraps of dew and dawn light,
a bullet-torn shroud of excelsior, scored
in dismal fire, levitating in the savage
Sabbath sky. By then, their mothers,

in the last moments of girlish rawboned glory,
appear in baggy, sky-blue prison shifts,
their beautiful hands lifting to shield their eyes,
like saints about to be slaughtered,

as if the light is too much, the sky suddenly egg-blue,
plaintive, threatening to pale away, the sun
still invisible, yet blinding. Barefoot, weepy,
they call their babies by name and secret endearment,

touch them everywhere like one might the awakened dead.
The children remain dignified, nearly aloof
in their perfect innocence and self-possession,
toddling dutifully into the arms of anyone

who reaches for them, even the guards, petting them too.
When visiting hours conclude, the children hand
their mothers cards and drawings, remnants
of a life they are too young to remember,

but conjure in glyphic crayon blazes.
Attempting to recollect the narrative
that will guide them back to their imagined homes,
the mothers peer from the pictures to the departing

children—back and forth, straining
to make the connection, back
and forth until the children, already fast asleep
as the bus spirits them off, disappear.

Raskolnikov

Ragged, head shaven, yellow
from months of cabbage
and cockroach soup, he arrived
on the transfer bus from Siberia.
The full lick is he offed a pawnbroker
and her sister, for no good reason,
then refused to cop a plea.
When he caught this jolt,
his old lady,
a beautiful chick named Sonya,
followed him all the way
from Saint Petersburg
to live in a trailer behind the quarry
so she can visit him
an hour and a half on Sundays.
He got put in an Honor Grade road gang
cutting right o'way for the tar squad
with a bush-axe—Number 2 Gained Time—
but he hacked off his toes,
one by one, for the hell of it.
The shrinks have their usual kicks
with this *phenomenon*,
but they are chilled by his Minnesota
Multiphasic Personality
Inventory, and he sees the Grand
Inquisitor in the Rorschachs.
They know he's not just another bughouse
John playing possum,
running the dozens.
"Goddam Russians,"
they sneer, throw him in Segregation
on a steady diet of Thorazine.

$\rightarrow$

25

First day back on the yard,
he gets written up for eating
tree bark and denouncing Chaplain Ray;
makes a bee-line for the fence;
then, climbing, gets hung up,
spread-eagled, concertina
jigging through his guts.
Beneath him convicts gather,
trying to say his name.

Praise the Lord

I was so new to North Carolina, I thought *The PTL Club* a satire, in the vein of *Saturday Night Live*. Jim and Tammy's spoof of televangelists was brilliant. I laughed—even after I found out the truth.

When I arrived at Heritage Village, the PTL compound, with five invited black felons, outfitted in forest green Honor Grade, the Bakkers met us in the parking lot. Sobbing, we lurched from the white prison van: the day before, two guys had been maced in it for pulling shivs and the fumes hadn't dissipated. Interpreting our tears for transports of the spirit, Jim and Tammy began to cry and took us, one by one, into their arms.

Their lavish grounds had an etched storybook opulence as if traced from a template and its colors coded in. As we strolled the packed studio, the guys affected, as they often did in public, a stoic gangster nobility—upon their faces a cross between glowering and bemusement, more than anything glad to be out of the joint for the afternoon, but ready to cut and run in a heartbeat.

At a predetermined time, the inmates were to exclaim ensemble, during the show, when the cue came: *Praise the Lord.* We rehearsed it a number of times. The guys loved seeing themselves on the monitors. They waved and mugged like kids. Then we were live: Jim's smile and big lapels, Tammy's face in the fiery stage lights, Andre Crouch and the Disciples singing gospel, a litany of *Praise the Lord* drizzling over the immense crowd.

We saw on the monitors what free folks at home saw as they watched us on TV in their living rooms: at intervals the inmates flashed among the mendicants like returned prodigals. Then: from the offstage sound man they received their cue. He held up finger number one, Jim suddenly holding the mike, like a torch, to their shocked faces as, on the count of three, each camera in the studio pivoted toward them.

→

They said nothing, neither smiled, nor moved—as if God, in His almighty wisdom, His good taste and discretion, His infinite love for the very least, had struck them stone.

Drayfer's Last Number

Let the Midnight Special
shine the ever-lovin' light on me.
                                    — Huddie Ledbetter (Leadbelly)

At the camp Christmas party in '76,
the whole population crowded into the chow-hall.
Local congregations, the Charlotte Council
on Alcoholism, the Council on Aging,

and Planned Parenthood chipped in.
The Church Women United fixed popcorn balls
and candy apples, punch
with ice cream floating in it.

The kitchen crew baked star cookies sparkled
scarlet and green. In the middle of each table,
bright oranges piled in tin chain gang bowls
haloed with plastic holly, red berries,

and a white candle. Chaplain Sinclair
from Poplar Tent delivered the invocation:
a few tremulous words about freedom and transgression.
It was in their power, those convicts, to do right.

Amnesty twinkled in the sky above the concertina.
The Christ child was birthed in a shack
no bigger than the hole.
There was a Jewish boy—he looked black—

→

from Ahoskie up in Hertford County:
Ira Dreyfuss—went by Drayfer.
He'd been struck blind while down
and wore a yarmulke.

Two cooks hoisted him up on the steam table,
handed him his guitar, a big silver nickel-
plated brass National Steel from the 20s,
palm trees, hummingbirds, and volcanoes

scored into the glory of its torso.
Silent Night, White Christmas, Jingle Bell Rock,
I'll Be Home for Christmas.
Drayfer could have been a free, seeing John on the lam.

His axe keened like a prowling wolf.
He played with a slide on his finger rigged
of a shin bone. His last number
was *The Midnight Special,*

a Leadbelly tune named after the train
that highballed by Sugarland Penitentiary
in Texas where Leadbelly had done time.
The legend went: if the Midnight Special

shined its light on a man, he'd be spirited
back to the free world—
about all a convict needed from Jesus,
the Midnight Special Himself.

The Bible was rife with unexpected fire.
As Drayfer neared the end, the men rose,
haltingly, one by one and sang along,
clean to the shimmering lick

of that last dwindling chord.
Drayfer was no boy at all.
Underside his forearm tracked blue numbers.
They all wore numbers.

Moonlite Avenue

Joan lived in a boxy mill house
on Moonlite Avenue where it leapt off the bottom
of Franklin Boulevard near the yarn mill.
Junkers chocked on blocks in dirt yards,

barking dogs staked to axles, dancing
in their mess. Men on slab carports,
out of work, cleaning shotguns.
Gastonia, North Carolina.

Convicts called it *Little Chicago*:
highest murder rate per capita in the U.S.
Joan worked at a camp for *youthful offenders*:
taught ABE, started a library, drove them

in the prison van to Friends House for rehab
and group, traveled to watch their games
in the prison league. Women are mystics
helping boys course the suffering rivers of their lives;

those children in the jailhouse—
they understood this perfectly.
They loved Joan, Our Lady of the Convicts.
Yet, a prison wall denies a woman.

It knows North and South,
East and West, brooks no heart,
save the heartless. The hawk-nosed
Captain, old-school chain gang, church

deacon, all that—decent enough, really,
though just couldn't get by the Bible:
It had driven a spike through the center of his brain,
wrapped him in concertina.

He believed she had no business on his prison yard.
Women stir a man toward freedom.
That kind of freedom, that kind of love, bleeds
into higher crimes, sin being sin.

The Sunday I visited Moonlite Avenue,
I accompanied her to First Baptist uptown—
the first Protestant church I had ever entered.
Apostate Catholic, in my last white shirt,

I was born in Pennsylvania where Quakers
chiseled prisons out of darkness and solitude.
As women do, she smoothed her dress
against the backs of her legs when she sat,

then dipped for the hymnal.
The minister wore a suit with the head
of a purple gladiola in its lapel.
He laid it out plain:

I was sitting in the seat of the scornful.
If I kept at the road I was on, no telling.
Like my first Sabbath out of the penitentiary,
I clasped Joan's hand.

Fair, she had to cover from the sun.
Above all she was modest, eyes blue as cotton—
my last stab at straight, at winning back everlasting.
I lifted my hymnal and sang with the rest—   →

like I was one of them, like I was saved—
about blood and the wages of sin.
She took me home to her table.
I slept in her bed beneath

the ponderous quilts of her ancestors.
Under her pillow snugged a .22 pistol;
on the nightstand, a red leather Bible,
a gift from her mother, inscribed

(December 24, 1967) John 14:14:
If ye shall ask anything in my name,
I will do it.
She barely knew me.

Angel

A boy at the Brunswick Camp
stuffed pillows under his prison greens,

duct-taped his arms and legs
with mattress batting, then crabbed

up the fence like a movie creature.
Hung in the wire all night, undetected,

a prehistoric scarecrow with wings,
spraddled cruciform,

until the dawn shift change.
When the sun sighted down,

the tower man shot him.
Feathers spooled out:

a living-barely grail of retribution,
hemorrhaging red feathers—

the flesh made word.
One is tempted to whisper *angel*—

one who'd done hole-time
in Deuteronomy,

dotty and vain,
bane and craven winsome,

riddler and cutter—
the worst of heretics,   →

Icarus or Lucifer, one, up there
in the coiled throes of concertina

swagging in the breeze;
then some kind of keen—

a wildcat screaming her heart out
—across the swales:

easy enough in the penitentiary
to breed myth and Bible.

ECO

(Ex-Convicts Organization)

Like *Echo*— though not the lovelorn
nymph of mythology—it perched
in the stained-glass attic alcove

of First Presbyterian, Trade
and Church Streets uptown.
Behind it brooded Old Settlers Cemetery,

the first selectmen to break land
in Mecklenburg County. Charlotte
was fertile ground for blue blood.

God invested in His sacred dead
upon which the living homeless
curled come night like salted slugs.

In the hushed cathedral nave
quaked a pew: *Stonewall Jackson*
bolted to a brass tablet. Whores fretted

beneath the clerestory windows,
burnished with Madonna and Child.
Two stories above, in the ECO office,

ex-cons—staggered mere moments
from the camps that turned them out
with a Greyhound ticket, their pittance

$\rightarrow$

parsed in Harris-Teeter sacks—
sat innocently on faded red velvet
window seats, waiting for the world

to quell their sorrow:
street clothes, a night or two
at Yokefellow, soup kitchen food.

Through a tiffany of St. George, horseback,
spearing a simpering dragon, whirled
the day's frenzy of light.

From the church cellar Art School
ascended the etudes of Piedmont Court
project kids plinking Chopin.

This Mad Heart

Rending this mad heart,
tearing it open...
        —Kim Chi-Ha, "By the Sea"

Often, after our days with the convicts
at Huntersville and Camp Greene,
Joan and I met at The Black Cat:
miso soup and Roastaroma mocha,
the verse of Kim Chi-Ha—whispered
love poems from a South Korean dungeon.

Everything was crucial: the pottery
from which we dined;
a two-women band (flute and viola);
the man, face caked with mime-white,
burlesquing astonishment, blue
angles above beady eyes, red
lip gloss bowing his girly mouth;
sculpted copper twisted into cleffs
espaliered on walls with Goya prints
and mimeographed handbills:
Echankar, Feldenkrais,
Transcendental Meditation.

We read *Soul on Ice*,
Soledad Brother, posted dues
to Charlotteans against the Death Penalty,
The North Carolina Prison and Jail Project,
The National Moratorium
on Prison Construction, subscribed
to *The Fortune News*, wrote letters
imploring the nation's governors

to spare their condemned, burned
candles outside the Death House in Raleigh.

Into the night we hit the Double Door
to hear George Thoroughgood
and the Delaware Destroyers
do John Lee Hooker. Small
and cruddy, so immovably packed
rowdy that patrons pissed
on the floor as they danced and drank
Schaeffer—*the one beer to have*
when you're having more than one—
the dive vibrated like a lame rocket
straining off the pad, all shudder
and torque, everyone shouting
against the revving amps:
One Bourbon, One Scotch, One beer—
until it crescendoed in the screeching electrons
of the band's red Fenders,
the drummer's signature 50 caliber tantrum;
then teasingly gyred down between last call
and encore, the Destroyers'
sweaty charade of departing the platform;
then re-ignition, *fizz* and *bam*:
their banner number—*Bad to the Bone*.
Toasting pitchers, busted glass
for another twenty minutes
until the overheads blazed on,
interrogatives of smoke
in the footlights where the band had been.

Joan and I spun onto Independence Boulevard.
The Head Shop's window swirled
glass bongs and crystal Buddhas.
From its jamb fanned clouds of reefer
and cloying strawberry incense.
Some Christer on the curb hawked nickel bags.
Harleys queued the sidewalk
outside Plumley's Pool Hall, Pagans
snorting long lines of coke
off black chopper saddles. Just a block away,
the cops hauled drunks into County Detox.
A populist peanut farmer
from Plains, Georgia was president.
Freaks and *Eraserhead* played at the Visulite.

Robert Lowell

I was a fire-breathing Catholic C.O,
and made my manic statement,
telling off the state and president, and then
sat waiting sentence in the bull pen
beside a Negro boy with curlicues
of marijuana in his hair.
       —*Robert Lowell,* "Memories of West Street and Lepke"

Mind-blown from maximum jolts
at Central Prison and outlying county gun camps,

shackled State felons, in felon brown,
huddle in the bullpen,

a caged room of church pews, awaiting process
into Honor Grade units across North Carolina.

Among them lounges the shade of Robert Lowell—
foggy, white as the Mayflower, goggled

in heavy black spectacles, snowy hair
spiriting about him like "curlicues

of marijuana." At the sound
of his blue-blooded Boston name—

Robert Traill Spence Lowell II—he rises
fettered with the patrician air of Caligula

tripping in his chains as if to his writing chair
to be mug-shot against the red felt

convict backdrop, a cameo
of numbers sprayed across his breast.

Waving a smoking Lucky,
dark eyes mirroring the manic glitter

of vermouth, he invokes
the Holy Ghost, blesses his fellow yard-birds

in a flaming hail of Gatling couplets.
They merely glance at him—

another Jailhouse poet, drafting
one more season of the manacle,

his final sentence on the State: Parnassus,
a road camp down-east, bedded

in the Green Swamp, where lurk
bear and panther. The last red wolf

scribbles stealthily in brack and fen,
never consenting to be seen again.

The Sick Room

It was used to lock convicts
waiting to see the nurse

and the climbers who got hooked
in the concertina

until the ambulance arrived.
A cot with a grey blanket,

tile floor, bars on the window.
Guards napped there between shifts.

It's where they dragged Juju,
thrashing like a sand shark,

leg irons ringing, the day
during Ramadan he ODed.

They stripped him to skivvies,
strapped him down with Sam Browns

from the Captain's office.
Just converted to Islam,

he'd been fasting. He looked starved.
Didn't open his eyes,

rolling under closed lids,
just bared his beautiful teeth

and tried to levitate
off the polyurethane mattress.

"Don't trust him," the guards warned me.
"If you met him on the street,

he'd cut your throat for your shoelaces."
But I hadn't met him on the street

where I never would have held his hand
and pleaded with him to tell me

what it was
he'd finally swallowed.

Prison AA

A retired guy from Charlotte
ramrods the meetings, every Monday
straps his Harley with coffee and doughnuts,
knifes up I-77 to Huntersville—
9 sharp in the Ed trailer
on the lip of the quarry.
"Hi. I'm Bill and I'm an alcoholic,"
he convenes each session.
"Hi, Bill," the convicts chorus,
whip out their laminated serenity prayers.

Bill's beat to hell from boozing.
You can see he didn't hold back.
But he has that second chance halo
hovering over his scruffy head.
He got sober just in time,
he confesses in his drunkalogue:
"sick and tired of being sick and tired."
Laid out on the sofa in his underwear,
he couldn't even hold a glass.
"One drink was too many
and a thousand not enough."
His wife fed him vodka with an eyedropper
to get him on his feet
so he could check into Black Mountain.
Now his whole life is the Program,
as many as three meetings a day.
He holds up seven years of chips
and the Big Blue Book.
"Doesn't matter what your higher power is,"
he testifies. "It can be a rock."

The guys light cigarette after cigarette,
smoke slashing between their teeth.
There's not much they don't know about getting wasted:
shoe polish, turpentine, Acqua Velva, deodorant.
Most of them were fucked up
the first time they went down—
then every other fucking time after.
Bill explains a drunk is always a drunk,
always recovering. Unrequited thirst,
yet to quench it is forbidden.

It's still early. Silver light
blooms in the concertina swaying
over the camp. Beyond it,
the free world walks a straight line.
There's a shared acknowledgment among the convicts,
pinched in little school desks,
that something's got to give or they'll die.
They can't live another day like this:
grown men in prison greens,
shuffling up once the meeting's over
to the coffee and doughnuts.
Week after week, they concur with everything
Bill says. A man's got to want to change.

Faccia Tosta

VISTAs didn't draw paychecks.
Volunteers in Service to America,
we signed on to live, theoretically,
like our clients—convicts
in North Carolina prisons.
Reimbursed for living expenses,
two grand a year seemed princely in '76,
the bicentennial year, two centuries
into the dream of riches and liberty
my grandparents from Foggia and Naples
had sailed into seven decades earlier.

I roomed with a Cuban exile
whose cleric father still wrote him in Spanish
from the Havana jail he'd been thrown in by Castro.
We lived on Central Avenue and split
the rent: $135.00, everything included.
We both drove VW bugs on the verge of collapse.
Our furniture was passed-along, third-hand, dickered-
for with a dandy thrift shyster, pearl-
handled derringers clipped on either jewel-
belted hip, and a peroxide wedge of pomade hair.
Our neighbors argued in Aramaic and Esperanto.
Every third night the cops shook down the whole complex,
and marched us out to the quad, cast iron
tables and chairs chained to stunted crepe myrtles
sprayed with the garish alphabet of despair.

Those were the facts I monthly spilled
to the welfare lady at DSS
when my number was called and I shambled
from the waiting room into her cubicle to be interviewed.

Hooded by her majestic Angela Davis afro,
she flashed me a ravishing smile.
She knew I was a fraud. Alone with her—
her mouth, her hair, her dark luscious otherness—
it was my first intimation of what it might be like
to cross love with a black woman.

I tiptoed from her office with a book of food stamps
like church raffle tickets, happy, I suppose,
to score them. I had no money, though
I felt anything but oppressed. Fugitive
from my former life, up North,
no one in Charlotte knew me.
It was safe to be poor and dirty and radical,
to declare prisons cruel and unusual punishment,
that the death penalty be abolished.

When my parents first visited me, my mother
insisted on cooking a big Italian meal.
At the grocery, I whipped out my food stamps.
Already suspicious of my neighborhood,
my Cuban roomie, Goodwill furniture,
the mattress on my bedroom floor,
the whole prison thing, she blanched.
I'd forgotten everything she and my father
had striven all their lives to teach me.

My forebears had lurched into America,
nothing but ocean in their amnesiac skulls
and a swart, black-maned brood of babies.
The only warmth, the only wealth, they harbored,
were the embers burning in their sockets,
evident in every crude photo that's survived.
And they had backbone, ramrod, rusted,

silent as ingots. They abandoned poor-mouth
to the jagged hills of Italy, huddling feverish
weeks in steerage on the beating Atlantic—
Guineas, Wops, Dagos—
then the Depression: *not a crust of bread,*
not even two nickels to rub together.
Seven kids on each side, eight
if you counted the dead. But they made do
and they stayed together. No welfare.

Faccia tosta, my ancestors hissed.
I knew what that meant: *a hard face.*
But, among my family, it really meant
a mask slipped on for the occasion:
the face of woe, or greed or even want—
a coward's untruth. *Disgrazia.*
You had to have a real face to grovel
handouts from a black woman
in the Relief Office down South—
after all my college, meted out
in paystubs my father climbed frozen
boom cranes on the open hearth for
and my mother, shackled to a sweatshop
Singer in a dim downtown tailor shop.

My stubble and ragged jeans, arty
consunto t-shirts. Masquerading
as a victim. My epic hardheaded ancestors—
they had broken their backs giving me
the luxury to pretend hunger was a game.
I had so much to eat, I begged for more.

Transfer Day

Tuesday the transfer bus
from Central Prison rumbles
through the camp's weedy gravel plot

to drop its new batch of Honor Grades:
some in irons, half-sedated, often
crazed, carrying their shriveled lot

in grocery bags and shoeboxes.
Like refugees, like a Jim Crow
newsreel of the chaingang diaspora,

they march fifty free feet
from the bus door to the prison gate:
into another stretch in a new warp,

hopefully the going-home end of their jolt,
each patted down tripping off the bus,
then again on the yard. Everyone armed.

A phalanx of guards on the ground
with shotguns; shotguns in the manned towers;
the ancient Lieutenant with an illegal pump-action.

Even the Captain leaves his office
strapped down to preside.
The delicacy is exquisite:

the intimacy. No way to gauge
what might trip a jackpot.
Now and then a boy just greening up

to Honor Grade from felon time,
and it's too much for him: the bold
blue ether, thrall of emerald just beyond

the fence, everything within reach.
A guard is not much different than a convict.
One hates the other, loves the other.

What's revealed in the way of distinction
is but the shade of their shirts.
The real danger comes when they're neither

one nor other. There is a running man.
There are guns and two different color shirts.
Mainly it's habit, inbred as incest.

Shank

The first shank
I was shown doubled

as a toothbrush,
the fiberglass

handle sharpened
to a pointed hush

by scraping it
on the concrete

cellblock floor.
Stick it in,

then pull it out
and scrub your teeth,

its owner confided.
Hygiene comes first in here.

That Good Old Way

Down in the river to pray, studying about that good old way
And who shall wear the starry crown, good Lord, show me the way
Oh sinners let's go down, let's go down, come on down
Oh sinners let's go down, down in the river to pray—
                                        —Traditional Appalachian Song

Fourth of July, the Church Women United
host an ice cream social for the men
doing time at Camp Greene.
Set up on the boiling yard: scored
cedar slab tubs, layers of ice
and rock salt. Hand-crank.
The old way. The good way.
Those women at the churns,
sweating like spike drivers, smiling
beneath the delirious sun, spoon
ice cream in Dixie cups from the prison canteen,
offer it to the inmates, take them into their embrace,
testifying: *Once you hit those streets,*
not a thing in the world say you can't do it.
We're praying for you. God loves you.
They come at them with Philippians 4:13:
I can do all things through Christ which strengtheneth me.
These men—they've pillaged and burned,
consorted with the Devil—possess nothing
to counter with, but sheepish *Yes, ma'ams.*
They have no scuffle with God.
Was the police locked them in the penitentiary.
In heavy state uniforms, weighted
with manacles of sweat,
the camp guards shy back.
Prisons don't suffer women gladly;

they're a threat to security.
But the Church Women,
cups of ice cream outstretched,
beckon them forth—they are powerless
to resist—and cleave them too
unto ample bosoms, assure them
that they as well have appointments in the Kingdom;
the Master is no respecter of persons.
For a moment, on a prison yard verged in fire,
convicts and keepers alike, both vilified
in the good book, are refreshed in the promise
that one day they'll be raveled back to the fold.
And when the women break into song,
they stumble along, whether they reckon the words
or not, as their ice cream melts.
Then they drink it down.

Cletis Pratt

And Samson said, Let me die with the
Philistines.
                    —Judges 16:30

First man I ever saw in irons,
wearing nothing but a pair of scurvy white
long john britches, was Cletis Pratt,
two guards, casually gripping his upper arms,
escorting him back to the population
after two weeks in single cell—same as the hole,
officially termed *Administrative Segregation.*
They had shaved his head.
He looked like Karl Marx.
He looked the wrath of Nazareth.
His big black beautiful beard
was nappy and clotted with what looked like lint,
but he had gone grey in the hole,
and fat with outrage, eating Thorazine and salt peter
(*Saint Peter* in the vernacular).
He'd never fooled around with weights,
had had a chiseled impossibly perfect onyx body,
where now pounded a gut
and two silver dugs.
Hobbled by a short span of chain
and two shackles, another chain
circling his waist to which his hands were buckled,
he couldn't quite keep up,
though the guards weren't hurrying him.
Sweating and winded, he bobbed and minced
like a dazed fighter—
too exhausted to lift his heavy hands to protect himself,
to ask for mercy, to just go down—

his first day back in the gym,
starting to train again
after a jolt in the penitentiary;
needles in North Charlotte;
needles on Hay Street in Fayetteville,
82nd Airborne, all the medals and insignia,
the Purple Hearts, his stunning beret.
Two tours in Vietnam.
Ten fucking lifetimes ago.

Recidivism

From the Latin: recidīvus *"recurring" and* recidō
"I fall back" and re *"back" and* cadō *"I fall."*
— Merriam-Webster Dictionary

Before working in a prison, I had never heard the term. A guard, Albert Overcash, took me out on escape with him—a violation that would've meant his job. Albert knew the guy on the run—Clarence Vessel (alias Weasel)—and didn't think it mattered one way or another if Clarence were caught or stayed gone. "I'm sure not hauling him back to the camp," Albert vowed.

Clarence, a revolving-door drunk, had never hurt anybody. They'd pick him up, drunker than ten men, for loitering or pissing against a dump-ster, stealing potted meat at Kroger. Give him eighteen months. He'd serve six active, bump out, then back in for Mogen David, Wild Irish Rose, MD 20-20. DTs, black-outs, his gray matter eaten up with rotgut.

Albert laid this all out to me. Before I knew anything. Before I had a notion of time and captivity. He didn't want to be a prison guard; but, my age, he had a wife and new baby girl. In high school, he had had a tryout with the Cubs, then got his girl pregnant and dropped out before graduation to work, copped a GED, and finally picked up the job at Huntersville Prison: simple enough if you could navigate the application and clear the PIN check. A shitty job with shitty wages, but stability and benefits. He was chipping away on a degree in Criminal Justice at Central Piedmont. He smoked reefer and drank malt liquor. Thin hair fell over his ears; he wore gold bracelets and necklaces with his uniform. The old guards didn't like him. He thought every last bit of it was a farce.

We just rode around the day Clarence Vessel ran, relieved we didn't run up on him. As dictated by procedure, Albert communicated over the CB to other vehicles involved in the chase: *10-4* and *What's your 20?* On his chest, he wore the silver Department of Correction nameplate: *M.A* (for Maynard Albert) *Overcash*. We crossed into Cabarrus County, stopped at a roadhouse for beer and corndogs, listened to Led Zeppelin, threw darts and drove back to the Unit.

I don't know if Clarence was ever found. 60 to 70 percent of the men and women sent up go back to prison at least once during their lives— not even taking into account the ones who never get out. Those numbers seemed so absurdly impossible that I dismissed them— Albert's kind of joke, a stab at irony. He worked third shift, all night— the dead man's shift—when the prison unleashed its haints and diabolical. He'd hole up in the sergeant's office, between the two wings of the cellblock, packed each with ninety convicts, bunked three-tiers high, some very dangerous men, and read Stephen King. Albert and I went to the Capri on opening night and watched *The Shining*. He insisted we sit in the first row. Those bloody, desiccated monsters hurtling through the screen into our faces. We were both twenty-three. He knew I was trying to be a writer. He had a drawer full of stories he promised to show me.

But for all that, he invested in the wrong person, forgot the first principle of his profession: never trust a convict. *Contraband* (another term): a buzz, some tiny shimmer to elevate Albert above the yard into the book he was dying to write—maybe about a young white prison guard with a new family who gets roiled up with a black convict cook, perhaps the two are secretly in love, and sells his soul for a weedy lid of dirt-clotted home-grown.

→

59

Albert got popped. Ended up trailing time himself at a minimum camp in Anson County: 6 months active—like Clarence Vessel. Often that's how it starts: a fellow catches piddling time behind an innocent high, wrong place, wrong time (same way Albert explained Clarence). Could happen to anybody: one lousy misfire and you find yourself a convict, sporting prison greens, in constant peril. Perhaps that life even becomes you.

After that first jolt, Albert flopped back and forth to the penitentiary, mainly possession and public drunks, dibbing and dabbing, and finally he ran. He's out there somewhere, right now, his name on a fugitive warrant.

Flate

His Christian name was Flate,
but they called him Flight, Fly mainly:
six-eight with hands so big, fingers so long,
they looked drawn-on by Romare Bearden.
He was black as Rhodesia,
and nobody, guard nor convict,
in the South Piedmont Area could even half-
shadow him on a hoop court.
He had had a full ride to Barber-Scotia
in Concord before he busted
into a funeral home, jonesing
for formaldehyde one night, and caught this time.
When Flate's five from the camp tar squad
played the guards at the old Huntersville High
gym, Sergeant Ford took Fly man
and they rigged a Box and One.
Ford was All-County at Garringer in '69,
but Fly was something extra-over.
Each time he schooled Ford,
the camp five keened like a choir, chanting
deathless junk that befuddled the guards.
Ford's screws threw their towels and insulted the ref.
They played dirty,
but the convicts took it.
Nothing they didn't know about dirty.
Fly never betrayed the game:
stuck to the facts, dribbled
like sharpening a shank.
The ball in his hand was a ripe, astonished peach.
It simply disappeared. His leap:

→

an exaggeration in the rafters,
all sky, then *whoom*:
two more for the bad guys.

South

That first Christmas, after four months
working a road camp prison north of Charlotte,
I caught a ride home to Pittsburgh
with a VISTA buddy. Before splitting,

we attended the camp's AA Christmas party:
cookies, carols, drunkalogues leavened
with mildness in deference to the season.
Mainly thankfulness, certain regret,

but all about regeneration:
how the path through sorrow had yielded
its portion of enlightenment.
Advent: dark and bitter cold

for North Carolina, for anywhere,
the first hours of what would prove
the fiercest winter in a hundred years.
When we hit Greensburg, PA,

the extent of my lift, I hopped out,
still 30 miles off, to thumb the rest of the way—
4:30 in the morning, 11 degrees—
among a pack of played-out stiffs,

on cardboard and rags beneath an overpass bridge,
struggling too to get somewhere for Christmas.
They wore the faces of time—
I had learned by then to divine it—

→

guys no longer astonished by how quickly
things go to the bad, who could weather it too,
so little to lose they didn't have to suffer
the likes of me. Hitchhiking

on the Pennsylvania Turnpike was against the law.
I riveted my eyes to the frozen right-o-way
and prayed for first light.
I rolled into the city in time for breakfast

in my parents' kitchen—
which sounds like the beginning of things.
During the holidays, I played poker,
drank a little beer, had final lunches

with a couple girls, read George Jackson,
Eldridge Cleaver, went to midnight Mass
with my parents. In my dad's mammoth Newport
I navigated a blizzard to a New Year's Eve party

at the Mardi Gras where a fight jumped off
and a Liberian Pinkerton opened a boy's head
with his stick, batted to pieces the jukebox,
then threw everyone out into the glowing

indifferent ice of 1977's inaugural morning.
I wrote long letters to Joan Carey,
back with her family in Georgia.
People asked how it was living down South.

There were a few jokes about prison,
but mainly no one wanted to know about it.
For the first time my life belonged to me
and I wanted to keep it secret: Joan

and our unheated attic, the candles;
standing in line with convicts
at the canteen for a cup of chicory,
the stink of the overheated cellblock,

prison cooks in whites frying
catfish in the chow-hall, flies year-round,
the yard snared in blinding concertina,
a slick of backwoods macadam jetting by

the cadaverous trailers on Mount Holly-
Huntersville Road where chain gang guards
once lived with their families. That winter,
as far as the gulf coast of Mississippi, it snowed.

Five-hundred-year-old live oaks
crashed to earth.
Slow rivers froze. Copperheads
furled deeper into the quick.

Home

Home is the place where, when you have to go there,
They have to take you in.
  —Robert Frost, "The Death of the Hired Man"

I whipped the Valiant onto Pegram Street
in North Charlotte, notorious
even among inmates, to visit the home
to which a certain convict would be paroled.

I had to make sure there was no opposition to his return,
verify transportation to and from his workplace,
that he at least had somewhere to eat and sleep
(not just the streets), that the folks he'd be living with

wouldn't feed him dope and booze
and right away drag him down,
that there existed some hope that this ex-con
might stay out of prison, support himself

without stealing or fighting,
that he might figure it out this time—
though less likely now after too many years in jails
to believe he could ever make it in the straight world.

The house was poor, one-story, paint-flaked slum.
Neighbors milled on their porches when they spied
the state automobile, yellow North Carolina
tag flaming off its rear bumper, then me

in my coat and tie trip over the curb and up
the rickety steps and knock on the door.
There was just a grandmother—no legs,
chopped off at the pelvis—fixed to a slab

of plywood on skates she rolled along
the floor with long brown fingers.
She had cleaned the house, set out tea
and little squares of cake, finger bowls

with tulip petals floating in them.
We talked about the boy coming home—Carl
(Coot on the yard). In prison,
he had adopted the Muslim name, *Mutasid Mohammed.*

He fasted and no longer ate pork.
Nation of Islam. *A Salaam el hakim.*
He carried a rug to pray to Allah on.
He'd been raised AME Zion.

The grandmother didn't know what she'd do with him.
She believed in the Bible.
She loved her grandson. Still, Coot,
or whoever he'd crossed over to, was now a man.

He had to find his own way to stay
out of the penitentiary. She guessed
she'd have to change too. Didn't matter
what God saved her boy.

Jury Duty

The defendant ran a meth lab out of his car.
So went the allegation.
He was a case study loser. State-raised,
I'd bet my right hand, the one I held up
when I swore to tell *the truth,*
or the left I laid upon the Bible,
the whole truth and even went so far
as *nothing but the truth.*
Jury wages were twelve dollars a day.
So help me God, there is no whole truth.

He had a bland surname
indigenous to the county, grand
in the original Saxon—*steed*
or *courage*, *blade*, perhaps *skill*—
but now meant little as the bailiff's shambling
at the DA's bidding. Just a dull scrape,
not a bit of music about it.

The judge told him to turn and face the jury
where we sat boxed on church benches.
He wore a white undershirt, jeans
and mangled Reeboks he had tarred in,
ill-fitting wool Hound's-tooth suit-coat,
dead of wet summer, cuffs short enough
to let trickle the tattoos: fabulous
blue and gold peacock feathers swirling
with eyes and planets, inked up and down
his forearms, as if secreted beneath his shirt
surged the entire maniacal bird.
Ash-blond dreadlocks pinned up like entrails.
Fettered hands. A shit-eating leer

he mistook for a smile—that certified his guilt.
Anybody would want to get rid of him,
send him up, see him dead.
He was genetically guilty,
DNA guilty. His whole life,
there hadn't been a lick of punishment he'd escaped—
whether they could find against him or not.
Next to his natty young Public Defender,
he looked even more criminal—
a staged illustration of counterpoint.

Felon time awaited him:
concurrent jolts, outstanding warrants,
fugitive papers. An orange jumpsuit
in the county jail, diagnostic
and classification, then a sojourn
in Central Prison, a year at least,
before farmed to some cliff-side gun camp
in Swain County to scrounge for Honor
Grade transfer who knows where—
a world away from home and family.
He'd been in and out his whole life;
he'd know what to do:
attend AA and NA meetings,
go to Wednesday Bible study in the chow-hall,
climb in the back of the prison van
once he was approved for Level II and truck off
to play putt-putt or swim at the Y, whatever
else he could manage. He'd take
every damn pledge available and mean it.
This time, he was going to do good when he got out.
He had never been bad, just a fuck-up,
an archetype, a mythic throwaway: predestined
or cursed, one—like Sisyphus, his scarred face

against the same mammoth stone that beat back
down over him every blessed time
he shoved it up the hill.

The DA, a big man, asked each of us in turn:
if we'd had earthly consort with the defendant,
if we had anything to do with crystal meth.
Then he made his pitch, what we had to keep in mind:
that the defendant was innocent
(which everyone knew was bullshit)
until proven guilty (the burden of such provenance
borne by the State). We the jurors
were to be unequivocally objective, weighing only
the factual evidence with which we'd be regaled.
Though objectivity, as it always is, was out
of the question the instant the jury laid eyes
upon the defendant whose only innocence resided,
as he stood before the jury—so terribly
different from us, so degenerate—in the way
loose strands from the quagmire on his head
fluttered in the breeze from the ceiling fans.

The DA then inquired—
he phrased it as a rhetorical question—
if we understood clearly that sympathy
of any sort (in this instance
for the defendant) should absolutely not
play a part in our deliberations.
Were we in agreement with that?
If not, we should so signify, and the Judge
would summarily ask us to step down.

That is when my hand
rose up from my body, like a fledgling
soul lamming out of Limbo,
and the DA leveled at me a face
that made me regret my hand,
striking out from me, as if entirely blameless,
not my hand at all, but a tidy scroll
of incontrovertible evidence—
that I could neither elude nor deny—
of my own guilt and certain punishment.

Teddy Bear

Hearing Harold Furr was the baddest
man in Huntersville Prison
was a revelation.
Pudgy, he had a beard that looped

like a horseshoe ear to ear,
a Conway Twitty pompadour,
and the mustache of a thirteen year old.
Nicknamed Teddy Bear,

he worked unit maintenance.
A smiling, round felon in green
fatigues and tool belt,
toting a ladder and can of WD-40,

he looked like my school janitor.
There's no real way to know
what a man is like by looking at him.
Baddest meant something,

but I didn't know what it meant.
How could I, a free man,
a school teacher, who knew when to lower
his eyes and walk away?

Still, in my romantic way,
I fancied myself a kind of outlaw
when after class Teddy and I sat
and talked at the yard picnic tables,

as if the world had done me wrong too.
To say he and I were friends is a stretch.
We got along just fine,
but I knew that if I so much as licked

a stamp for him, he'd have me.
Paroled, he rented a place,
unbelievably, at the bottom of my street.
Occasionally I'd spy him,

shirt unbuttoned on his big white belly,
walking Freedom Drive
home from his job at Gordy Tire.
I'd stop and give him a lift.

Things were going okay.
"Nothing to it," he'd brag,
with a big hairy smile.
I'd drop him at the little bungalow

he was fixing up.
He always shook my hand,
told me I was "good people," and invited me
to a standing Friday night poker game.

Every Friday I thought of showing up,
becoming one of them, a man
who could gut out anything:
a jolt in prison, the hell kicked out of him,

the grease and bust of working with his back
for grub wages, chain-smoking and drinking
cheap beer in simmering danger,
bluffing a whole table of ex-cons and bikers

out of a jackpot. But, in truth,
I'm not such a man.
Yet all my life,
I've had to convince myself of this.

Affronted or wounded, I plot revenge,
but it's merely rhetorical.
Mostly I brood.
It would not cross my mind to shoot someone.

I've never fired a gun of any sort.
Teddy, on the other hand,
must have offended the wrong person;
it's pathetically easy to accomplish:

bump a bet once too often,
rat-hole your winnings,
pull up stakes prematurely.
You might even good-naturedly remark

at another's unusual luck,
scrape a pot to your chest with too much relish.
The list is endless and capricious.
You are completely unaware

that you've slighted anyone.
People grin boozily, shake hands
and assure you they enjoyed it;
they'll see you next Friday.

But when you're asleep they return—
not merely in your dreams—
but through the front door and that's that:
a convoy of screaming police cruisers

strobing blue the predawn street,
yellow vinyl crime tape
winding around the pine trees
in Teddy's front yard.

Poetry

I died in 1960 from a prison sentence and poetry
brought me back to life.

— Etheridge Knight

(For Rebecca Gould Gibson)

A poet at a Quaker college,
Rebecca Gibson has never entered a prison.
A silent guard escorts her by elevator
down below the earth, as if time-

traveling—steel box in a steel house:
knobless, slick on all sides, controlled
by an invisible hand and disembodied voice
snapped over an intercom.

Like an alluring saint traipsing
into a leper hospital—
that luminous feminine detachment—
she is led to a room: a long wooden

table and chairs, closed circuit
cameras in cornices. Barred window:
halogen orbs strobe the sky,
swirling shadows of concertina,

swooning search lights
sweep the perimeter.
A dozen convicts in felon brown
sit around the table, State tablets

and sharpened #2 Ticonderogas.
Rebecca speaks about the heartbreak
of family, its disorder and turmoil;
then reads her poems: "[marveling]

at the persistent love /
the only paradise we'll ever know,"
how, "Again, we fail to connect."
The guys signify, deeply into it.

They place together their palms,
close their eyes, drop their heads.
She confesses that she wants to feed them poems,
implores them to be honest.

They write about longing and children,
women and God, of their crimes,
what they'll do differently, how they know,
now, behind this wall of sentences,

what it takes to make it on Earth.
These men pull ferocious time:
life to die. Underground.
They'll never get out.

They've done the terrible things inked in their files.
Shrouds of threadbare light,
the dying light of hope,
envelop them: hope—

that the same blameless words
that tripped and seared them,
pulled triggers, drove steel into flesh;
words that masqueraded as their lives,

then died in their arms, and finally
chained them to this cellar—
that those very words, spilled tonight
as poetry, will be enough to pluck them

from the penitentiary.
When Rebecca rises to depart,
they stand, receive her proffered hand,
look into her eyes, she into theirs—

the light rimes her as well—and she wonders
aloud in breathtaking innocence
if parole boards ever listen to poems,
an interrogative blazing

for an instant in the shaft of night:
a poem trembling in a convict's
hand as he stumbles over his own syllables,
the incredulity of the parole board,

their heads cocked, hearing
something so unimaginable, so
numinous, they're evangelized.
There would be that same reel of light,

the convict absolved, loosed to black January,
stationed beyond the wall, awaiting him,
with such cold precision. Tonight.
Outside the door burn legions of time.

Inmates Working

An orange diamond highway sign,
color of the sun rising, proclaims

in black: *Inmates Working*.
The white prison van, silver state tags,

steel slabs ramparting its windows,
parks in a ditch of fugitive daffodils.

In Department blue blouse and trousers,
the driver walks shotgun.

Convicts—in fluorescent orange vests,
stenciled *INMATE*, over felon brown—

comb the road for clues of the lives
they've departed, jabbing the earth

with spiked sticks. About them,
wheat grows. Fog speaks;

they are not alone. Like doppelgängers,
gray on black and diaphanous,

their dead convict ancestors, booted
two by two and stripe-wearing, beat

silently with bushaxes the underworld weeds.
These spirits take nothing, leave nothing.

They no longer make time here.
Just their dawn kin, corporeal, illuminated,

spearing into pumpkin orange trash bags
the shoulder's pact of glass and paper, flesh.

The City Jail

The City Jail spiked out of Fifth Avenue
in the heart of downtown Pittsburgh.
When we drove by it, my father would pause
and signify in its direction,
never uttering a word. Riding shotgun,
my mother on cue blurted she'd glimpsed
our imaginary condemned prisoner
in the jail's uppermost barred window.
From his cell, four stories high, he looked down
and spied me. Dressed in drab fatigues—
like Duquesne Light's meter reader
who snuck through the alley with his tablet,
tallying each spark of power we consumed—
he waited to be strapped in the electric chair.

In the back seat with my sister—mesmerized
by Dickens, so good she had no worries
about retribution—I craned up to see him
and exclaimed, though I can't fathom why,
There he is.
My mother, unblinking, pursed mouth,
eyebrows fixed like an empress's,
looked at me as if to say:
Yes, of course, he's there
and now you've seen him.

For a boy like me—
straight F's in Christian Doctrine,
scarlet U's in conduct,
a boy who faced at best hard time
in Purgatory—the meaning jails held
was abundantly clear.

There were places if you faltered: Juvie,
Thorn Hill, Morganza, St. Joseph's
Military Academy. Bread and water,
rubber hoses. Guards and guns,
ropes and chains—crueler than nuns,
darker than confessionals.
They'd come and take you away,
give you the electric chair, the gas chamber.
They'd chop your head off.

I was certain I'd never escape the City Jail,
my next detention after maxing out
of the 19th century brick schoolhouse
in which, day after day, I built time,
parsing venial from mortal before bearing
false witness about my sins to the Jesuit
in his long black cassock and purple stole.
I made the Sign of the Cross when passing
the jail, like passing a cathedral—
some small indulgence in it, I prayed, perhaps
a notch or two, off my sentence—
bowing my head, hammering my heart.
Mea maxima culpa.
It truly was my most grievous fault—
whatever I had done.

It was just a game—about the man
in the jail window—a terrifying game,
like catechism, the adults admired—
to turn you good—their wizened parable.
My parents thought me merely playing along,
like claiming to have witnessed my guardian
angel, or Santa beating it up the flue,
simply trying to please them—

not that the true reckoning of that man
on Fifth Avenue enveloped me
in black, like the last smoky flicker
swinging on its drowning taper-wick.
They'd break into smiles,
Marie's head dipped back to *Bleak House.*
There was nothing to be afraid of.

Years later, I would leave my parents and sister,
slip silently out of my father's Chrysler
into my own car and steer it out of Pittsburgh,
South, to work in a prison, past the City Jail
where that man still draped his window,
longing for the executioner's hood
to drop over his head. Occasionally,
I'd see him, bone-shackled, straddling
a ditch along a Carolina county roadbed, swinging
a bushaxe, pounding bedrock to ash.
He had the addled ice eyes of the lightning-
struck, crosshairs stitched on his forehead.
He never failed to recognize me.

Three Little Pigs

Helms—a common name in the Piedmont—
I carried him in the State Valiant to interview

work-release for a barbeque-cook's job
in his hometown, a seam of forgetful brick

buildings on Hwy. 52 in Rowan County
between two frontiers of pine green

grass slope and swift clear water,
cows, a few white sheep, maybe three

horses, brown with latches of white
vertical on their brows,

every so many miles a sudden cap of granite
jutting out of the swales. Then suddenly

you're right up on it: feed store, café, railhead,
post office, bank, a Pure Station, cafe,

antique store with antebellum china
sitting on antimacassars

in the front window. Still stenciled
on the calcified heirloom brick, stubbled

with mortar for all the times it was repointed,
ever-fading ads for Piedmont cigarettes

and Blenheim's Ginger Ale,
big checkerboards of Purina.

Modest clapboard homes, trim yards,
rural PO routes. A gauntlet of churches.

A man hosed the sidewalk of the storefront
barbeque house on Main Street.

Three smiling girl pigs, wearing crowns
and petticoats, cloven hooves

nail-polished red, danced like the Rockettes
on a crude mural above the awning.

A wolf in a top hat loomed above them,
mouth watering, wringing his claws

in carnal anticipation. Helms
hadn't even changed clothes for the interview.

Came out of the camp kitchen,
untying his nasty apron.

But the rest of him was tailor-made, bonaroo:
white tucked t-shirt, black belt, white cuffed pants,

then the high black polished chain gang clodhoopers,
white soda jerk hat. Pack of Camels,

parceled up, square as a city John, high
in his sleeve. A smoke between his lips.

Scraggly mustache. Red hair, pink face.
The boss never stopped hosing,

quizzed Helms right there on the street.
Got himself the job without ever walking in the joint.

Knew every blessed angle of BBQ:
fire, wood, temperature, tomato

vs. vinegar, pork vs. beef, pits
vs. smokers, white vs. red slaw,

rolls vs. hushpuppies, chopped vs. sliced,
heirloom sauces, family secrets,

clandestine recipes.
He knew the songs. By God,

he knew the pigs. Like it was holy writ.
Like he was no convict at all.

Huron Valley

Oversized Royal blue snap-blouses,
matching trousers, orange stripes
flowing at the outseam—

big bags of time to shrink them,
circled in little yellow chairs,
eyes closed, listening as Trudy

recites by heart the poems
she refuses to commit to paper.
Words are contraband the man spins

into more time: sentences,
stanzas, entire volumes:
the signed confession of her life.

Beneath a tired red wig,
lily tat on her jugular,
she rhymes in toothless hip-hop.

The best relationship she'd had
in years was with her pimp;
she liked not thinking for herself.

Her daughter was murdered
outside Motown Kabob.
Mama died since she's been down.

Now, behind this time,
all she does is ponder walls
of words immuring her.

These women know whoring in Detroit:
signify like church, amen Trudy
when her voice breaks,

hand around the circle a roll
of toilet paper, tearing off spans
to dab their eyes. Through a window,

in the corridor, a male guard
occasionally peeks in at them. Outside
invisible through the valley slices

the Huron River. Along its banks
flare purple crocuses, straining to open—
to make it back—this wintry April.

Certainty

Far from home—penniless,
food stamps, everything
from Goodwill—I lived with Joan Carey,
a Baptist girl from Tucker, Georgia.

For eighty bucks, we leased a Charlotte attic
across from Detox and Memorial Stadium,
and worked in the prisons.
My family in Pittsburgh wondered what I was doing

for no wage, and why,
all the way down in North Carolina—
like some agitator.
The certainty I lived in then

made me happier than I've ever been.
One torrid August night, 3 a.m.:
we barged out of a party at the Weavers'.
Joan and I and Jim, our VISTA boss.

We had come in Jim's tiny Honda:
brown, homely, tires the size of saucers.
We were headed for Krispy Kreme
up on Independence,

the *Hot Doughnuts Now* neon
about to announce yet another epiphany
in that enchanted tropical August.
Joan was twenty:

sundresses I remember like pets from my childhood.
And Jim: so young and confident.
Inside they danced to Thelma Houston's
"Don't Leave Me This Way,"

setting fire to hallelujah—
the last sacrifice of summer.
Hearts and windows shattered across the Queen City.
Glad to be together,

we stepped into the street toward the car.
The night was far from over.
Yet up in the huge magnolias,
early morning cast its thermal hush

upon the revel. The three of us
saw it at the same time:
Jim's Honda, somehow detached
from its station at the curb,

rolled down the middle of 8th Street.
An automobile inexplicably animated
with sinister purpose—as if we'd tripped
unwittingly through the scrim

segregating us from that other world
where things happen for no reason at all.
Jim and I intercepted it, backpedalling
as it bulled us toward the intersection,

until we finally halted it inches from catastrophe.
We looked at one another and laughed—
the way convicts ambling Huntersville yard
laughed about building thirty-forty years

in the penitentiary.
Guys my age who wouldn't see the streets again,
until after the sons Joan and I would one day parent
had grown into men and left home.

The laugh Joan and I exchange all too often
when the unimaginable
hurtles into an otherwise placid day.
The laugh I think of now as fear.

Huntersville Prison

When finally, after thirty-six years,
I return to Huntersville Prison

to document that it actually existed—
is not merely a litany of rectitude

I chant inside my head like a celled monk—
it's been razed. All that marks it

is a span of innocent chain link, concertina
spooling to rust on its sagging spine.

Prom kids lark here to vamp
in its spooky caprice—

like an abandoned morgue or sanitarium—
what they imagine of bedlam's pleasures.

Surveyor stakes spike along the vanished front gate.
Ditch witches and backhoes hulk,

hemmed by berms sown in pink grading flags.
The yard's been bulldozed,

scraped of artifacts, except for a single brick,
and latch of mangled iron with which

I draw in the dust a child's diagram:
the Captain's office, its museum of contraband;

his concubine, the secretary, astride him
with her crossword puzzles; the yard

phone booths where convicts hunkered feeding
the black engines dime after dime, listening

to familiar voices withering in the wires;
the chow hall; cell block; Ed Trailer; cook

and maintenance shacks; canteen hoop
court; horseshoe pit; and finally the hole,

a barred confessional over which the guard tower
lorded its searchlight and bored 20 gauge.

It's smaller—my prison;
isn't that what's always said of the past?

Its remorseless efficiency.
Shrunken. Abstracted. Synopsized.

Vectors of time sweep this plat
of anguish. They're building

houses here, the yard soon to be held
in families, children wandering this earth—

fronting the quarry (future marina),
its fathomless green glaze

the apocryphal grave of entire chain gangs
heaved off its granite chin. Even

the massive elms that shaded the picnic tables
where Sundays the men received their kin

have disappeared. Dirt is not permitted
the amnesty of forgetfulness.

It nurtures curse. It broods and worries.
I close my eyes and wave that manacle.

For an instant my prison roils to life—
like a reliquary quickening

on a martyred saint's feast day.
Convicts fade in and out, stick figures,

scratches in the dust, smoky filaments
in the cracked documentary of time.

Sentence after sentence trails off
into the elliptical void: years to days, hours

pared to minutes, down to the second,
the inverse of everlasting.